ATOM-SMASHING
POWER OF MIND

T0145904

Also available in the Condensed Classics Library

A MESSAGE TO GARCIA

ACRES OF DIAMONDS

ALCOHOLICS ANONYMOUS

AS A MAN THINKETH

ATOM-SMASHING
POWER OF MIND

HOW TO ATTRACT
GOOD LUCK

HOW TO ATTRACT MONEY

POWER & WEALTH

PUBLIC SPEAKING TO WIN!

SELF-RELIANCE

THE ART OF WAR

THE GAME OF LIFE AND
HOW TO PLAY IT

THE KYBALION

THE LAW OF SUCCESS

THE MAGIC LADDER
TO SUCCESS

THE MAGIC OF BELIEVING

THE MASTER KEY
TO RICHES

THE MASTER MIND

THE MILLION DOLLAR
SECRET HIDDEN IN
YOUR MIND

THE POWER OF AWARENESS

THE POWER OF
CONCENTRATION

THE POWER OF YOUR
SUBCONSCIOUS MIND

THE PRINCE

THE PROPHET

THE RICHEST MAN
IN BABYLON

THE SCIENCE OF
BEING GREAT

THE SCIENCE OF
GETTING RICH

THE SECRET DOOR
TO SUCCESS

THE SECRET OF THE AGES

THINK AND GROW RICH

THINK YOUR WAY
TO WEALTH

WALDEN

YOUR FAITH IS YOUR
FORTUNE

ATOM-SMASHING POWER OF MIND

by Charles Fillmore

The Life-Changing Classic on Your Power Within

Abridged and Introduced
by Mitch Horowitz

THE CONDENSED CLASSICS LIBRARY™

MEDIA

Published by Gildan Media LLC
aka G&D Media.
www.GandDmedia.com

Atom-Smashing Power of Mind was originally published in 1949
G&D Media Condensed Classics edition published 2019
Abridgement and Introduction copyright © 2019 by Mitch
Horowitz

FIRST PRINT AND EBOOK EDITION: 2019

Cover design by David Rheinhardt of Pyrographx

Interior design by Meghan Day Healey of Story Horse, LLC.

ISBN: 978-1-7225-0219-5

Contents

Introduction
Charles Fillmore:
The Man Who Never Stood Still
by Mitch Horowitz 9

Chapter One
The Atomic Age 13

Chapter Two
The Restorative Power of Spirit 21

Chapter Three
Spiritual Obedience 27

Chapter Four
I AM or Superconsciousness 31

CHAPTER FIVE
Day of Judgment 37

CHAPTER SIX
Thou Shalt Decree a Thing 39

CHAPTER SEVEN
Thinking in the Fourth Dimension 43

CHAPTER EIGHT
Is This God's World? 47

CHAPTER NINE
Truth Radiates Light 51

CHAPTER TEN
The Only Mind 57

CHAPTER ELEVEN
The Body 63

CHAPTER TWELVE
Faith Precipitations....................................... 69

CHAPTER THIRTEEN
The End of the Age 71

ABOUT THE AUTHORS 77

Charles Fillmore:
The Man Who Never Stood Still
By Mitch Horowitz

Spiritual experimenters through the ages, from ancient astrologers and alchemists to contemporary chaos magicians and mind-power mystics, have always availed themselves of the latest technologies of their eras. The New Thought pioneer Charles Fillmore, who founded the vibrant and ongoing Unity movement, was a great example of this.

Born in 1854 on an Indian reservation near St. Cloud, Minnesota, Fillmore and his wife and intellectual partner Myrtle, organized their Kansas City-based Unity ministry into one of the nation's first mass-media ministries. As early as 1907, the Fillmores staffed phone banks with round-the-clock volunteers ready to assist callers with distance prayers. The Unity ministry made early use of radio, targeted mailings, correspondence courses, pamphlets, and well-produced magazines aimed at the large demographic range of Unity's congregants. This included the children's monthly *Wee Wisdom*, which launched the literary career of best-selling novelist Sidney Sheldon when it published the ten-year-old's first poem in 1927.

Up to the eve of his death in 1948, Charles Fillmore remained well versed in the science and technology of the newly dawned atomic era. Fillmore sought to unite the insights of science and practical mysticism in the collection of writings that make up *Atom-Smashing Power of the Mind*, which appeared the year after his death.

This 1949 book is one of Fillmore's finest literary efforts. It serves as a powerful and stirring summation of his theology of mind-power metaphysics. At the same time, Fillmore relates the higher abilities of thought to the revolutions in atomic energy that entered public awareness in the years immediately preceding his death. Of this, Fillmore makes a creditable effort, foreseeing future developments in wireless, microwave, and cellular technology. When I consider my failings to stay fully versed in the digital technology of our own era, I am all the more admiring of a frontier boy who grew up not only to establish a major religious denomination but who never stopped learning about the radically changing world around him. Within those changes, Fillmore discovered confirmation of his own universal ideals.

This condensation of *Atom-Smashing Power of Mind* captures the verve, spirit, and soaring language of his original, while retaining his key points and practical insights. I consider Fillmore's book one of the finest mid-century statements of New Thought philosophy. It is the kind of work that should inspire those of us today who believe that all knowledge—scientific, technological, psychological, medical, and spiritual—ultimately converge. Of this, Charles Fillmore was absolutely certain.

Chapter One

The Atomic Age

The majority of people have crude or distorted ideas about the character and the location of Spirit. They think that Spirit plays no part in mundane affairs and can be known by a person only after his death.

But Jesus said, "God is Spirit;" He also said, "The kingdom of God is within you." Science tells us that there is a universal life that animates and sustains all the forms and shapes of the universe. Science has broken into the atom and revealed it to be charged with tremendous energy that may be released and be made to give the inhabitants of the earth powers beyond expression when its law of expression is discovered.

Jesus evidently knew about this hidden energy in matter and used His knowledge to perform so-called miracles.

Our modern scientists say that a single drop of water contains enough latent energy to blow up a ten-story building. This energy, existence of which has been discovered by modern scientists, is the same kind of spiritual energy that was known to Elijah, Elisha, and Jesus, and used by them to perform miracles.

By the power of his thought Elijah penetrated the atoms and precipitated an abundance of rain. By the same law he increased the widow's oil and meal. This was not a miracle—that is, it was not a divine intervention supplanting natural law—but the exploitation of a law not ordinarily understood. Jesus used the same dynamic power of thought to break the bonds of the atoms composing the few loaves and fishes of a little lad's lunch—and five thousand people were fed.

Science is discovering the miracle-working dynamics of religion, but science has not yet comprehended the dynamic directive power of man's thought. All so-called miracle workers claim that they do not of themselves produce the marvelous results; that they are only the instruments of a superior entity. It is written in I Kings, "The jar of meal wasted not, neither did the cruse of oil fail, according to the word of Jehovah, which he spake by Elijah." Jesus called Jehovah Father. He said, "The works that I do in my Father's name, these bear witness of me."

Jesus did not claim to have the exclusive supernatural power that is usually credited to Him. He had explored the ether energy, which He called the "kingdom of the heavens;" His understanding was beyond that of the average man, but He knew that other men could do what He did if they would only try. He encouraged His followers to take Him as a center of faith and use the power of thought and word. "He that believeth on me, the works that I do shall he do also; and greater works than these shall he do."

Have faith in the power of your mind to penetrate and release the energy that is pent up in the atoms of your body, and you will be astounded at the response. Paralyzed functions anywhere in the body can be restored to action by one's speaking to the spiritual intelligence and life within them. Jesus raised His dead bodies in this way, and Paul says that we can raise our body in the same manner if we have the same spiritual contact.

What have thought concentration and discovery of the dynamic character of the atom to do with prayer? They have everything to do with prayer, because prayer is the opening of communication between the mind of man and the mind of God. Prayer is the exercise of faith in the presence and power of the unseen God. Supplication, faith, meditation, silence, concentration, are mental attitudes that enter into and form part of prayer. When one understands the spiritual character of God and adjusts himself mentally to the omnipresent God-Mind, he has begun to pray rightly.

Audible prayers are often answered but the most potent are silently uttered in the secret recesses of the soul. Jesus warned against wordy prayers—prayer uttered to be heard of men. He told His disciples not to be like those who pray on the housetop. "When thou prayest, enter into thine inner chamber, and having shut thy door, pray to thy Father who is in secret, and thy Father who seeth in secret shall recompense thee."

The times are ripe for great changes in our estimate of the abiding place and the character of God. The six-day creation of the universe (including man) described in Genesis is a symbolic story of the work of the higher realms of mind under divine law. It is the privilege of everyone to use his mind abilities in the superrealms, and thereby carry out the prayer formula of Jesus: "Seek ye first his kingdom, and his righteousness; and all these things shall be added unto you."

Of all the comments on or discussions of the indescribable power of the invisible force released by the atomic bomb none that we have seen mentions its spiritual or mental character. All commentators have written about it as a force external to man to be controlled by mechanical means, with no hint that it is the primal life that animates and interrelates man's mind and body.

The next great achievement of science will be the understanding of the mental and spiritual abilities latent in man through which to develop and release these tremendous electrons, protons, and neutrons secreted in the trillions of cells in the physical organism.

Here is involved the secret, as Paul says, "hid for ages and generations . . . which is Christ [superman] in you, the hope of glory." It is through release of these hidden life forces in his organism that man is to achieve immortal life, and in no other way. When we finally understand the facts of life and rid our minds of the delusion that we shall find immortal life after we die, then we shall seek more diligently to awaken the spiritual man within us and strengthen and build up the spiritual domain of our being until, like Jesus, we shall be able to control the atomic energy in our bodies and perform so-called miracles.

The fact is that all life is based upon the interaction between the various electrical units of the universe. Science tells us about these activities in terms of matter and no one understands them, because they are spiritual entities and their realities can only be understood and used wisely by the spiritually developed man. Electricians do not know what electricity is, although they use it constantly. The Christian uses faith and gets marvelous results, the electrician uses electricity and also gets marvelous results, and neither of them knows the real nature of the agent he uses so freely.

The man who called electricity faith doubtless thought that he was making a striking comparison when in fact he was telling a truth, that faith is of the mind and it is the match that starts the fire in the electrons and protons of innate Spirit forces. Faith has its degrees of voltage; the faith of the child and the faith of the most powerful spiritual adept are far apart in their intensity and results. When the trillions of cells in one's body are roused to expectancy by spiritual faith, a positive spiritual contact results and marvelous transformations take place.

Sir James Jeans, the eminent British scientist, gives a prophecy of this in one of his books. He says in substance that it may be that the gods determining our fate are our own minds working on our brain cells and through them on the world about us.

This will eventually be found to be true, and the discovery of the law of release of the electronic vitality wrapped up in matter will be the greatest revelation of all time.

When we awake to the fact that every breath we draw is releasing this all-potent electronic energy and it is shaping our lives for good or ill, according to our faith, then we shall begin to search for the law that will guide us aright in the use of power.

Chapter Two

The Restorative Power of the Spirit

Not only our Bible but the scriptures of all the nations of the world testify to the existence of an invisible force moving men and nature in their various activities. Not all agree as to the character of this omnipresent force, universal Spirit, but it serves the purpose of being their god under whatever name it may appear. Different nations ostensibly believe in the same scriptures, but they have various concepts of the universal Spirit; some conceive it to be nature and others God. Robert Browning says, "What I call God . . . fools call Nature."

Our Bible plainly teaches that God implanted in man His perfect image and likeness, with executive ability to carry out all the creative plans of the Great Architect. When man arrives at a certain point in spiritual understanding it is his office to cooperate with the God principle in creation.

As the animating life of all things God is a unit, but as the mind that drives this life He is diverse. Every man is king in his own mental domain, and his subjects are his thoughts.

People in this atomic-age civilization ask why God does not reveal Himself now as He did in Bible days. The fact is that God is talking to people everywhere, but they do not understand the message and brush it aside as an idle dream. We need to divest ourselves of the thought that Daniel and Joseph, in fact all the unusually wise men of the Bible, were especially inspired by God, that they were divinely appointed by the Lord to do His work. Everything points to their spiritual insight as the result of work on their part to that end.

The body is the instrument of the mind, and the mind looks to the Spirit for its inspiration. Not only the Scriptures that we look to for authority in our daily living but also the experience of ourselves and our neighbors proves that those who cultivate communion with the Father within become conscious of a guiding light, call it what you will.

Those who scoff at this and say that it is all the work of the imagination are deluding themselves and ignoring a source of instruction and progress that they need above all things. If this sense world were the only world we shall ever know, the attainment of its ambitions might be sufficient for a man of meager outlook and small capacity, but the majority of us see ourselves and the world about us in a process of transformation that will culminate in conditions here on the earth far superior to those we have imagined for heaven.

Jesus was very advanced, and His radiant body was developed in larger degree than that of anyone in our race, but we all have this body, and its development is in proportion to our spiritual culture. In Jesus this body of light glowed "as he was praying." Jesus' body did not go down to corruption, but He, by the intensity of His spiritual devotion, restored every cell to its innate state of atomic light and power. When John was in the state of spiritual devotion Jesus appeared to him, "and his eyes were as a flame of fire; and his feet like unto burnished brass." Jesus lives today in that body of glorified electricity in a kingdom that interpenetrates the earth and its environment. He called it the kingdom of the heavens.

We do not have to look to the many experiences recorded in the Bible of the spiritually illumined to prove the existence of the spiritual supersubstance. People everywhere are discovering it, as they always have in every age and clime.

The metaphysical literature of our day is very rich with the experiences of those who have found through various channels the existence of the radiant body. This prompts me to tell of my development of the radiant body, during half a century's experience. It began when I was mentally affirming statements of Truth. Just between my eyes, but above, I felt a "thrill" that lasted a few moments, then passed away. I found I could repeat this experience with affirmations. As time went on I could set up this "thrill" at other points in my body and finally it became a continuous current throughout my nervous system. I called it "the Spirit" and found that it was connected with a universal life force whose source was the Christ. As taught in the Bible, we have through wrong thinking and living lost contact with the parent life. Jesus Christ incarnated in the flesh and thereby introduced us by His Word into the original Father life. He said, "If a man keep my word, he shall never taste of death." I have believed that and affirmed His words until they have become organized in my body. Sometimes when I make this claim of Christ life in the body I am asked if I expect to live always in this flesh. My answer is that I realize that the flesh is being broken down every day and its cells transformed into energy and life, and a new body is being formed of a very superior quality. That new body in Christ will be my future habitation.

I have found that the kingdom of God is within man and that we are wasting our time and defeating the work of the Spirit if we look for it anywhere else.

Chapter Three

Spiritual Obedience

Zeal is the great universal force that impels man to spring forward in a field of endeavor and accomplish the seemingly miraculous. It is the inward fire that urges man onward, regardless of the intellectual mind of caution and conversation.

Zeal should be tempered with wisdom. It is possible to be so zealously active on the intellectual plane that one's vitality is consumed and there is nothing left for spiritual growth. "Take time to be holy." Never neglect your soul. To grow spiritually you should exercise your zeal in spiritual ways.

Above all other Bible writers Paul emphasizes the importance of the mind in the transformation of character and body. In this respect he struck a note in religion that had been mute up to this time; that is, that spirit and mind are akin and that man is related to God through his thought. Paul sounds again and again in various forms this silent but very essential chord in the unity of God and man and man and his body.

When the scientific world investigates the so-called miracles of religion and discovers that they are being duplicated continually, the power of mind over matter will be heralded as of great importance to both religion and science.

Prayer gives spiritual poise to the ego, and it brings forth eternal life when spiritually linked with the Christ. "If a man keep my word, he shall never see death."

To one who gains even a meager quickening of the Spirit, Christianity ceases to be a theory; it becomes a demonstrable science of the mind.

We must not anticipate better social and economic conditions until we have better men and women to institute and sustain those conditions.

Jesus said that He was the bread and substance that came down from heaven. When will our civilization begin to realize and appropriate this mighty ocean of substance and life?

A finer civilization than now exists has been conceived by many from Plato in his "Republic" to Edward Bellamy in "Looking Backward." But a new and higher civilization will be developed only through the efforts of higher and finer types of men and women. Philosophers and seers have looked forward to a time when this earth would produce superior men and women, but save Jesus none has had the spiritual insight to declare, "Verily I say unto you, This generation shall not pass away, until all these things be accomplished."

"Behold, the man!" Jesus Christ is the type of a new race now forming in the earth. Those who incorporate into consciousness the Christ principles are its members.

The dominion that God gave to man in the beginning, as recorded in Genesis, is a dominion over spiritual ideas, which are represented in the allegory by material symbols.

Hence to exercise his dominion man must understand the metaphysical side of everything in existence.

Divine Mind is the one and only reality. When we incorporate the ideas that form Divine Mind into our mind and persevere in those ideas, a mighty strength wells up within us. Then we have a foundation for the spiritual body, the body not made with hands, eternal in the heavens. When the spiritual body is established in consciousness, its strength and power is transmitted to the visible body and to all the things that we touch in the world about us.

In the economy of the future man will not be a slave to money. Humanity's daily needs will be met in ways not now thought practical.

In the new economy we shall serve for the joy of serving, and prosperity will flow to us and through us in rippling streams of plenty. The supply and support that love and zeal set in motion are not yet largely used by man, but those who have tested this method are loud in their praise of its efficiency.

Chapter Four

I AM or Superconciousness

Superconciousness is the goal toward which humanity is working. Regardless of appearances there is an upward trend continually active throughout all creation. The superconsciousness is the realm of divine ideas. Its character is impersonal. It therefore has no personal ambitions; knows no condemnation; but is always pure, innocent, loving, and obedient to the call of God.

The superconsciousness has been perceived by the spiritually wise in every age, but they have not known how to externalize it and make it an abiding state of consciousness. Jesus accomplished this, and His method is worthy of our adoption, because as far as we know, it is the only method that has been successful. It is set forth in the New Testament, and whoever adopts the life of purity and love and power there exemplified in the experiences of Jesus of Nazareth will in due course attain the place that He attained.

Jesus acknowledged Himself to be the Son of God. Living in the superconsciousness calls for nothing less on our part than a definite recognition of ourselves as sons of God right here and now, regardless of appearances to the contrary. We know that we are sons of God; then why not acknowledge it and proceed to take possession of our God heirdom? That is what Jesus did in the face of the most adverse conditions. Conditions today are not so inertly material as they were in Jesus' time. People now know more about themselves and their relation to God. They are familiar with thought processes and how an idea held in mind will manifest itself in the body and in affairs; hence they take up this problem of spiritual realization under vastly more favorable conditions. An idea must work out just as surely as a mathematical problem, because it is under immutable law. The factors are all in our possession, and the method was demonstrated in one striking instance and is before us. By following the method of Jesus and doing day-by-day work that comes to us, we shall surely put on Christ as fully and completely as did Jesus of Nazareth.

The method by which Jesus evolved from sense consciousness to God consciousness was, first, the recognition of the spiritual selfhood and a constant affirmation of its supremacy and power. Jesus loved to make the highest statements: "I and the Father are one." "All authority hath been given unto me in heaven and on earth." He made these statements, so we know that at the time He was fully aware of their reality. Secondly, by the power of His word He penetrated deeper into omnipresence and tapped the deepest resources of His mind, whereby He released the light, life, and substance of Spirit, which enabled Him to get the realization that wholly united His consciousness with the Father Mind.

In the light of modern science the miracles of the Bible can be rationally explained as Mind acting in an omnipresent spiritual field, which is open to all men who develop spiritually. "Ye who have followed me, in the regeneration when the Son of man shall sit on the throne of his glory, ye also shall sit upon twelve thrones, judging the twelve tribes of Israel."

"He that overcometh, I will give to him to sit down with me in my throne."

Overcoming is a change of mind from error to Truth. The way of overcoming is first to place one's self by faith in the realization of Sonship, and second, to demonstrate it in every thought and act.

The Word is man's I AM. The Holy Spirit is the "outpouring" or activity of the living Word. The work of the Holy Spirit is the executive power of Father (mind) and Son (idea), carrying out the creative plan. It is through the help of the Holy Spirit that man overcomes. The Holy Spirit reveals, helps, and directs in this overcoming. "The Spirit searcheth all things, yea, the deep things of God." It finally leads man into the light.

Science rightly understood is of inestimable value to religion, and Christianity in order to become the world power that its founder envisioned, must stress the unfoldment of the spiritual mind in man in order that he may do the mighty works promised by Jesus.

When Jesus went up into the mount to pray He was transfigured before His apostles Peter, James, and John. True prayer brings about an exalted radiation of energy, and when it is accompanied by faith, judgment, and love, the word of Truth bursts forth in a stream of light that, when held in mind, illumines, uplifts, and glorifies.

Jesus recognized Mind in everything and called it "Father." He knew that there is a faith center in each atom of so-called matter and that faith in man can move upon the faith center in so-called matter and can remove mountains.

Jesus taught that the realities of God are capable of expression here in this world and that man within himself has God capacity and power. Jesus was crucified because He claimed to be the Son of God. Yet the

Scriptures, which the Pharisees worshiped, had this bold proclamation, which Jesus quoted to them from Psalms 82:

"I said, Ye are gods,
And all of you sons of the Most High."

The reports by His followers of what He taught clearly point to two subjects that He loved to discourse upon. The first was the Son of God: He was the Son of God. Secondly: We might all become as He was and demonstrate our dominion by following Him in the regeneration.

In order to follow Jesus in the regeneration we must become better acquainted with the various phases of mind and how they function in and through the body.

In spiritual understanding we know that all the forces in the body are directed by thought and that they work in a constructive or a destructive way, according to the character of the thought. Medicine, massage, and all the material means accomplish but incomplete, unsatisfactory, temporary results, because they work only from the outside and do not touch the inner springs that control the forces. The springs can only be touched by thought. There must be a unity between the mind of man and Divine Mind so that ideas and thoughts that work constructively unto eternal life may be quickened in the mind and organism of man.

We are told in John that the world could not contain the books that would be written if all the things that Jesus did were put into writing. But enough is given in the story of His life and in the writings of the apostles concerning Him to bear witness to that which is daily being revealed in this day of fulfillment. Those who are consecrated to Truth and fully resolved to follow Jesus all the way are spiritualizing the whole man, including the body, which is being redeemed from corruption. Those who are living as Jesus lived are becoming like Him. "God is not the God of the dead, but of the living." Resurrection takes place in people who are alive.

CHAPTER FIVE

The Day of Judgment

It is said we are to be judged after death according to deeds done in the body, which are kept on record like books that are balanced; and if the balance is found to be in our favor we go up, and if against us we go down. But if we are spiritual now—divine—this spiritual part has dominion, and we begin to exercise this dominion. The moment we catch sight of this we begin to judge. We begin to put the thoughts that are good on the right and the others on the left. All our ideas of the attributes of our divine self we put on the right hand of power, while the thoughts of disease, death, limitation and lack we put on the left—denied, cut off.

This is not to occur after death. It is to begin right now!

Now is the time to plant the seed thought of the conditions we desire by saying, "Come my good thoughts, let us inherit our kingdom."

We do not fear anything, for we have separated our sheep from our goats; we have set our true thoughts on the right and have denied our error thoughts any power whatever.

Come into the kingdom of mind. Here everything that is in Principle is yours.

Everything, all good, is to be gathered up, and everything is good at its center. The essence of your body is good and of true substance. When you sift your consciousness of all but the real and true, the body becomes full of light.

The diamond owes its brilliance to the perfect arrangement of the innumerable little prisms within it, each of which refracts the light of the other. Man's body is made up of centers of consciousness—of light—and if arranged so they radiate the light within you, you will shine like the diamond. All things are in the consciousness and you have to learn to separate the erroneous from the true, darkness from light. The I AM must separate the sheep from the goats. This sifting begins right now and goes on until the perfect child of God is manifest and you are fully rounded out in all your Godlike attributes

Chapter Six

Thou Shalt Decree a Thing

To decree with assurance is to establish and fix an ideal in substance. The force behind the decree is invisible, like a promise to be fulfilled at a future time; but it binds with its invisible chains the one who makes it. We have only a slight conception of the strength of the intangible. We compare and measure strength by some strong element in nature. We say "strong as steel." But a very little thought will convince us that mental affirmations are far stronger than the strongest visible thing in the world. The reason for this is that visible things lack livingness. They are not linked with energy and intelligence as are words. Words charged with power and intelligence increase with use, while material things decrease.

It is not necessary to call the attention of metaphysicians to the fact that all visible things had their origin in the invisible. The visible is what remains of an idea that has gradually lost its energy. Scientists say that this so-called solid earth under our feet was once radiant substance. Nothing is really "solid" but the atomic energy latent in everything. They tell us that it takes some six billion years for uranium to disintegrate and become lead, and this rate of disintegration has helped scientists determine the age of the earth as about two billion years.

Since nothing is lost in the many transformations that occur in nature, what becomes of the energy that is being released in the disintegration that is going on in our earth? The answer is that a new earth is being formed in which matter will be replaced by atomic energy. This process of refining matter into radiant substance is taking place not only in the natural world but in our bodies also. In fact the speed with which the transformation takes place depends on the character of the thoughts that we project into our brains and through them into our bodies and the world about us. This is why we should spiritualize our thoughts and refine the food we eat to correspond.

At the present writing there is a housing shortage everywhere and the lack of materials and competent labor indicate that several years will elapse before the need is met. This is counted a calamity; but is it? The inventive genius of man is planning houses of glass and other materials that will be much less expensive—more durable and in every respect superior to the present homes. When man gets his ingenious mind into action he always meets every emergency with something better. Every adverse situation can be used as a spur to urge one to greater exertion and the ultimate attainment of some ideal that has lain dormant in the subconsciousness.

Chapter Seven

Thinking in the Fourth Dimension

Scientists tell us that the discoveries that their efforts are revealing convince them that they are just on the verge of stupendous truths. Christianity spiritually interpreted shows that Jesus understood the deeper things of God's universe. He understood exactly what the conditions were on the invisible side of life, which is termed in His teaching the "kingdom of God" or the "kingdom of the heavens." We are trying to connect His teaching with modern science in order to show the parallel; but as He said in Mark 4:23, "if any man hath ears to hear, let him hear." This means that we must develop a capacity for understanding in terms of the atomic structure of the universe.

Unless we have this spiritual capacity we do not understand. We think we have ears, but they are attuned to materiality. They do not get the radiations from the supermind, the Christ Mind. Physiology working with psychology is demonstrating that hearing and seeing can be developed in every cell in the body, independent of ears and eyes. We hear and see with our minds working through our bodies. This being true, the capacity to hear may extend beyond the physical ear into the spiritual ethers, and we should be able to hear the voice of God. This extension of hearing is what Jesus taught. "If any man hath ears to hear, let him hear."

Then we are told that we must "take heed" what we hear. Many of us have found that as we develop this inner, spiritual hearing, we hear voices sometimes that do not tell the truth. These deceptive voices can be hushed by affirming the presence and power of the Lord Jesus Christ.

As you unfold your spiritual nature, you will find that it has the same capacity for receiving vibrations of sound as your outer, physical ear has. You do not give attention to all that you hear in the external; you discriminate as you listen. So in the development of this inner, spiritual ear take heed what you hear: discriminate.

Jesus said, "For he that hath, to him shall be given: and he that hath not, from him shall be taken away even that which he hath." How can what a man has not be taken away? We believe in our mortal consciousness that we have attained a great deal, but if we have not this inner, spiritual consciousness of reality our possessions are impermanent. Then we must be careful what we accumulate in our consciousness, because "he that hath, to him shall be given." The more spiritual Truth you pile up in your mind, the more you have of reality, and the larger is your capacity for the unlimited; but if you have nothing of a spiritual character, what little you have of intellectual attainment will eventually be taken away from you.

The mysteries of the supermind have always been considered the property of certain schools of occultists and mystics who were cautious about giving their truths to the masses for fear that in their ignorance these might misuse them. But now the doors are thrown wide open, and whosoever will may enter in.

Our attention in this day is being largely called to the revolution that is taking place in the economic world, but a revolution of even greater worth is taking place in the mental and spiritual worlds. A large and growing school of metaphysicians has made its advent in this generation, and it is radically changing the public mind toward religion. In other words, we are developing spiritual understanding, and this means that religion and its sources in tradition and in man are being inquired into and its principles applied in the development of a new cosmic mind for the whole human family.

Chapter Eight

Is This God's World?

W hy doesn't God do something about it?"
This oft-repeated query, uttered by the
skeptical and unbelieving, is heard day in
and day out. Imitating the skeptics, Christian believ-
ers everywhere are looking to God for all kinds of
reforms in every department of manifest life and also
are charging Him with death and destruction the world
over.

One who thinks logically and according to sound
reason wonders at the contradictions set up by these
various queries and desires.

Is God responsible for all that occurs on this earth,
and if not all, how much of it?

The Bible states that God created the earth and
all its creatures, and last of all man, to whom He gave
dominion over everything. Observation and experience prove that man is gaining dominion over nature

wherever he applies himself to that end. But so much remains to be gained, and he is so small physically that man counts himself a pygmy instead of the mental giant that he is.

All the real mastery that man attains in the world has its roots in his mind, and when he opens up the mental realm in his being there are no unattainables. If the conquests of the air achieved in the last quarter century had been prophesied, the prophets would have been pronounced crazy. The fact is that no one thinking in the old mind realm can have any conception of the transformation of sound waves into electromagnetic waves and back again into words and messages of intelligence. Edison admitted that his discovery of the phonograph was an accident and that he never fully understood how mechanical vibrations could be recorded and be reproduced in all forms of intelligent communication.

Now that man has broken away from his limited visualizations and mentally grasped the unhampered ideas of the supermind, he is growing grandly bold and his technical pioneers are telling him that the achievements of yesterday are as nothing compared to those of tomorrow. For example, an article by Harland Manchester condensed in the *Reader's Digest* from *Scientific American* tells of the "microwaves" that are slated for a more spectacular career in the realm of the unbelievable than anything that has preceded them. This article describes in detail some of the marvels that will evolve out of the utilization of microwaves, among which may be mentioned "private phone calls by the hundreds of thousands sent simultaneously over the same wave band without wires, poles or cables. Towns where each citizen has his own radio frequency, over which he can get voice, music, and television, and call any phone in the country by dialing. Complete abolition of static and interference from electrical devices and from other stations. A hundred times as much 'space on the air' as we now have in the commercial radio band. A high-definition and color television network to cover the country. And, perhaps most important of all, a nation-wide radar network, geared to television, to regulate all air traffic and furnish instantaneous visual weather reports to airfields throughout the land."

Add to this the marvels promised by the appliers of atomic energy and you have an array of miracles unequaled in all the bibles of all the nations of the world.

It is admitted by those who are most familiar with the dynamic power of these newly discovered forces that we do not yet know how to protect our body cells from the destructiveness of their vibrations. Very thick concrete walls are required to protect those who experiment with atomic forces. One scientist says that the forces released from the bombs that were used on the Japanese cities in 1945 may affect those who were subjected to them and their descendants for a thousand years. Experimentation proves that we have tapped a kingdom that we do not know how to handle safely.

CHAPTER NINE

Truth Radiates Light

Spiritual light transcends in glory all the laws of matter and intellect. Even Moses could not enter the Tabernacle when it was aglow with this transcendent light.

It is written that the Israelites did not go forward on days when the cloud remained over the Tabernacle, but when the cloud was taken up they went forward. This means that there is no soul progress for man when his body is under the shadow of a "clouded" mind, but when the cloud is removed there is an upward and forward movement of the whole consciousness (all the people).

We are warned of the effect of thoughts that are against or opposed to the commandments of Jehovah. When we murmur and complain we cloud our minds, and Divine Mind cannot reach us or help us. Then we usually loaf until something turns up that causes us to think on happier things, when we go forward again.

Instead of giving up to circumstances and outer events we should remember that we are all very close to a kingdom of mind that would make us always happy and successful if we would cultivate it and make it and its laws a vital part of our life. "The joy of Jehovah is your strength."

You ask, "How can I feel the joy of Jehovah when I am poor, or sick, or unhappy?"

Jesus said, "Come unto me, all ye that labor and are heavy laden, and I will give you rest."

Here is the first step in getting out of the mental cloud that obscures the light of Spirit. Take the promises of Jesus as literally and spiritually true. Right in the midst of the most desperate situation one can proclaim the presence and power of Christ, and that is the first mental move in dissolving the darkness. You cannot think of Jesus without a feeling of freedom and light. Jesus taught freedom from mortality and proclaimed His glory so persistently that He energized our thought atmosphere into light.

The Scriptures state that when Moses came down from Mount Sinai with the Ten Commandments his face shone so brilliantly that the Children of Israel and even Aaron, his own brother, were afraid to come near him until he put a veil over his face. The original Hebrew says his face sent forth beams or horns of light.

The Vulgate says that Moses had "a horned face;" which Michelangelo took literally, in his statue of Moses representing him with a pair of horns projecting from the head. Thus we see the ludicrous effect of reading the Bible according to the letter.

Our men of science have experimented with the brain in action, and they tell us that it is true that we radiate beams when we think. The force of these beams has been measured.

Here we have further confirmation of the many statements in the Bible that have been taken as ridiculous and unbelievable or as miracles.

Persons who spend much time in prayer and meditate a great deal on spiritual things develop the same type of face that Moses is said to have had. We say of them that their faces fairly shine when they talk about God and His love. John saw Jesus on the island of Patmos, and he says, "His countenance was as the sun shineth in his strength."

I have witnessed this radiance in the faces of Truth teachers hundreds of times. I well remember one class lesson during which the teacher became so eloquent that beams of light shot forth from her head and tongues of fire flashed through the room, very like those which were witnessed when the followers of Jesus were gathered in Jerusalem.

We now know that fervent words expressed in prayer and song and eloquent proclamations of spiritual Truth release the millions of electrons in our brain cells and through them blend like chords of mental music with the Mind universal.

This tendency on our part to analyze and scientifically dissect the many supposed miracles recorded in the Bible is often regarded as sacrilegious, or at least as making commonplaces of some of the very spectacular incidents recorded in Scripture.

In every age preceding this the priesthood has labored under the delusion that the common people could not understand the real meaning of life and that they should therefore be kept in ignorance of its inner sources; also that the masses could not be trusted with sacred truths, that imparting such truths to them was like casting pearls before swine.

But now science is delving into hidden things, and it is found that they all arise in and are sustained by universal principles that are open to all men who seek to know and apply them.

Anyone who will search for the science in religion and the religion in science will find that they harmonize and prove each other. The point of unity is the Spirit-mind common to both. So long as religion assumes that the Spirit that creates and sustains man and the universe can be cajoled and by prayer or some other appeal can be induced to change its laws, it cannot hope to be recognized by those who know that unchangeable law rules everywhere and in everything.

Again, so long as science ignores the principle of intelligence in the evolutionary and directive forces of man and the universe, just so long will it fail to understand religion and the power of thought in the changes that are constantly taking place in the world, visible and invisible.

Chapter Ten

The Only Mind

I say, "An idea comes to me." Where did it come from? It must have had a source of like character with its own. Ideas are not visible to the eye, they are not heard by the ear, nor felt, nor tasted, yet we talk about them as having existence. We recognize that they live, move, and have being in the realm that we term mind.

This realm of mind is accepted by everybody as in some way connected with the things that appear, but because it is not describable in terms of length, breadth, and thickness, it is usually passed over as something too vague for consideration.

But those who take up the study of this thing called mind find that it can be analyzed and its laws and modes of operation understood.

To be ignorant of mind and its laws is to be a child playing with fire, or a man manipulating powerful chemicals without knowing their relation to one another. This is universally true; and all who are not learning about mind are in like danger, because all are dealing with the great cause from which spring forth all the conditions that appear in the lives of all men and women. Mind is the one reservoir from which we draw all that we make up into our world, and it is through the laws of mind that we form our lives. Hence nothing is as important as a knowledge of mind, its inherencies, and the mode of their expression.

The belief that mind cannot be understood is fallacious. Man is the expression of mind, dwells in mind, and can know more clearly and definitely about the mind than the things that appear in the phenomenal world.

Mind is the great storehouse of good from which man draws all his supplies. If you manifest life, you are confident that it had a source. If you show forth intelligence you know that somewhere in the economy of Being there is a fount of intelligence. So you may go over the elements that go to make up your being and you will find that they draw their sustenance from an invisible and, to your limited understanding, incomprehensible source.

This source we term Mind, because it is as such that our comprehension is best related to it. Names are arbitrary, and we should not stop to note differences that are merely technical. We want to get at the substance which they represent.

So if we call this invisible source Mind it is because it is of like character with the thing within our consciousness that we call our mind. Mind is manyfold in its manifestations. It produces all that appears. Not that the character of all that appears is to be laid to the volition of Mind; no, but some of its factors enter into everything that appears. This is why it is so important to know about Mind, and how its potentialities are made manifest.

And this is where we have set up a study that makes of every atom in the universe a living center of wisdom as well as life and substance.

We claim that on its plane of comprehension man may ask the atom or the mountain the secret that it holds and it will be revealed to him. This is the communication of mind with Mind; hence we call Mind the universal underlying cause of existence and study it from that basis.

God is Mind, and man made in the image and likeness of God is Mind, because there is but one Mind, and that is the Mind of God. The person in sense consciousness thinks he has a mind of his own and that he creates thought from its own inherent substance. This

is a suppositional mind that passes away when the one
and only real Mind is revealed. This one and only Mind
of God that we study is the only creator. It is that which
originates all that is permanent; hence it is the source
of all reality. Its creations are of a character hard for the
sense man to comprehend, because his consciousness
is cast in a mold of space and time. These are change-
able and transient, while the creations of the one Mind
are substantial and lasting. But it is man's privilege
to understand the creations of the one Mind, for it is
through them that he makes his world. The creations of
the one Mind are ideas. The ideas of God are potential
forces waiting to be set in motion through proper for-
mative vehicles. The thinking faculty in man is such a
vehicle, and it is through this that the visible universe
has existence. Man does not "create" anything if by this
term is meant the producing of something from nothing; but he does make the formless up into form; or
rather it is through his conscious cooperation that the
one Mind forms its universe.

Mind is the storehouse of ideas. Man draws all his
ideas from this omnipresent storehouse. The ideas of
God, heaven, hell, devils, angels, and all things have
their clue in Mind. But their form in the consciousness
depends entirely upon the plane from which man draws
his mental images. If he gets a "clue" to the character

of God and then proceeds to clothe this clue idea with images from without, he makes God a mortal. If he looks within for the clothing of his clue idea he knows God to be the omnipresent Spirit of existence.

So it is of the utmost importance that we know how we have produced this state of existence which we call life; and we should be swift to conform to the only method calculated to bring harmony and success into our life, namely to think in harmony with the understanding derived from communion with the God-Mind.

CHAPTER ELEVEN

The Body

You see at once that man is not body, but that the body is the declaration of man, the substantial expression of his mind. We see so many different types of men that we are bound to admit that the body is merely the individual's specific interpretation of himself, whatever it may be. Man is an unknown quantity; we see merely the various ideas of man expressed in terms of body, but not man himself. The identification of man is determined by the individual himself, and he expresses his conception of man in his body.

Some persons have tall bodies; some have short ones. Some have fat bodies; some have slim ones. Some have distorted bodies, some have symmetrical ones. Now, if the body is the man, as claimed by sense consciousness, which of these many bodies is man?

The Bible declares that man is made in the "image" and after the "likeness" of God. Which of the various bodies just enumerated is the image and likeness of God?

Let us repeat that the body of man is the visible record of his thoughts. It is the individual's interpretation of his identity, and each individual shows in his body just what his views of man are. The body is the corporeal record of the mind of its owner, and there is no limit to its infinite differentiation. The individual may become any type of being that he elects to be. Man selects the mental model and the body images it. So the body is the image and likeness of the individual's idea of man. We may embody any conception of life or being that we can conceive. The body is the exact reproduction of the thoughts of its occupant. As a man thinks in his mind so is his body.

You can be an Adam if you choose, or you can be a Christ or any other type of being that you see fit to ideate. The choice lies with you. The body merely executes the mandates of the mind. The mind dictates the model according to which the body shall be manifested. Therefore as man "thinketh within himself [in his vital nature], so is he." Each individual is just what he believes he is.

It is safe to say that nine hundred and ninety-nine persons out of every thousand believe that the resurrection of the body has something specifically to do with the getting of a new body after death; so we find more than ninety-nine per cent of the world's population waiting for death to get something new in the way of a body. This belief is not based on the principles of Truth, for there is no ready-made-body factory in the universe, and thus none will get the body that he expects. Waiting for death in order to get a new body is the folly of ignorance. The thing to do is to improve the bodies that we now have; it can be done, and those who would follow Jesus in the regeneration must do it.

The "resurrection" of the body has nothing whatever to do with death, except that we may resurrect ourselves from every dead condition into which sense ignorance has plunged us. To be resurrected means to get out of the place that you are in and to get into another place. Resurrection is a rising into new vigor, new prosperity; a restoration to some higher state. It is absurd to suppose that it applies only to the resuscitation of a dead body.

It is the privilege of the individual to express any type of body that he sees fit to ideate. Man may become a Christ in mind and in body by incorporating into his every thought the ideas given to the world by Jesus.

Divine mind has placed in the mind of everyone an image of the perfect-man body. The imaging process in the mind may well be illustrated by the picture that is made by light on the photographic plate, which must be "developed" before it becomes visible. Or man's invisible body may be compared to the blueprint of a building that the architect delivers to the builder. Man is a builder of flesh and blood. Jesus was a carpenter. Also He was indeed the master mason. He restored the Lord's body ("the temple of Jehovah") in His mind and heart (in Jerusalem).

The resurrection of the body is not dependent for its demonstration on time, evolution, or any of the man-made means of growth. It is the result of the elevation of the spiritually emancipated mind of the individual.

Step by step, thought added to thought, spiritual emotion added to spiritual emotion—eventually the transformation is complete. It does not come in a day, but every high impulse, every pure thought, every upward desire adds to the exaltation and gradual personification of the divine in man and to the transformation of the human. The "old man" is constantly brought into subjection, and his deeds forever put off, as the "new man" appears arrayed in the vestments of divine consciousness.

How to accomplish the resurrection of the body has been the great stumbling block of man. The resurrection has been a mere hope, and we have endeavored to reconcile a dying body with a living God, but have not succeeded. No amount of Christian submission or stoical philosophy will take away the sting of death. But over him who is risen in Christ "death no more hath dominion."

CHAPTER TWELVE

Faith Precipitations

When asked what electricity is, a scientist replied that he had often thought of it as an adjunct to faith, judging from the way it acts. This linking of faith and electricity seems at first glance fantastic, but when we observe what takes place when certain substances in solution and an electric current are brought in conjunction, there seems to be a confirmation of the Scripture passage: "Now faith is assurance of things hoped for."

Just as the electric current precipitates certain metals in solution in acid, so faith stirs into action the electrons of man's brain; and acting concurrently with the spiritual ethers, these electrons hasten nature and produce quickly what ordinarily requires months of seedtime and harvest.

Speedy answers to prayer have always been experienced and always will be when the right relations are established between the mind of the one who prays and the spiritual realm, which is like an electrical field. The power to perform what seems to be miracles has been relegated to some God-selected one; but now we are inquiring into the law, since God is no respecter of persons, and we find that the fulfillment of the law rests with man or a group of men, when they quicken by faith the spiritual forces latent within them.

The reason why some prayers are not answered is lack of proper adjustment of the mind of the one who prays to the omnipresent creative spiritual life.

Jesus was the most successful demonstrator of prayer of whom we have any record, and He urged persistence in prayer. If at first you don't succeed, try, try again. Like Lincoln, Jesus loved to tell stories to illustrate His point, and He emphasized the value of persistence in prayer. He told of a woman who demanded justice of a certain judge and importuned him until in sheer desperation he granted her request.

Every Christian healer has had experiences where persistent prayer saved his patient. If he had merely said one prayer, as if giving a prescription for the Lord to fill, he would have fallen far short of demonstrating the law. Elijah prayed persistently until the little cloud appeared or, as we should say, he had a "realization;" then the manifestation followed.

Chapter Thirteen

The End of the Age

In all ages and among all people, there have been legends of prophets and saviors and predictions of their coming.

The fact that all who believe in the principle of divine incarnation have long strained their eyes across the shining sands in an effort to catch sight of the coming of one clothed with the power of heaven, should make us pause and consider the cause of such universality of opinion among peoples widely separated. To dismiss the subject as a religious superstition is not in harmony with unprejudiced reason. To regard these prophecies merely as religious superstitions rules out traditions that are as tenable and as reliable as the facts of history. There is a cause for every effect, and the cause underlying this almost unanimous expectation of a messiah must have some of the omnipresence of a universal law.

In considering a subject like this, which demonstrates itself largely on metaphysical lines, it is necessary to look beyond the material plane to the realm of causes.

The material universe is but the shadow of the spiritual universe. The pulsations of the spiritual forces impinge upon and sway men, nations, and planets, according to laws whose sweep in space and time is so stupendous as to be beyond the ken or comprehension of astronomy. But the fact should not be overlooked that higher astronomy had its votaries in the past. The Magi and the illumined sages of Chaldea and Egypt had astronomical knowledge of universal scope. It was so broad, so gigantic, so far removed from the comprehension of the common mind of their day that it always remained the property of the few. It was communicated in symbols, because of the poverty of language to express its supermundane truths. In the sacred literature of the Hindus are evidences of astronomical erudition covering such vast periods of time that modern philosophers cannot or do not give them credence, and they are relegated to the domain of speculation rather than of science. However the astronomers of the present age have forged along on material lines until now they are beginning to impinge upon the hidden wisdom of the mighty savants of the past.

There is evidence that proves that the ages of the distant past knew a higher astronomy than do we of this age, and that they predicted the future of this planet through cycles and aeons—its nights of mental darkness and the dawn of its spiritual day--with the same accuracy that our astronomers do its present-day planetary revolutions.

Jesus evidently understood the aeons or ages through which earth passes. For example, in Matthew 13:39, our English Bible reads: "The enemy that sowed them is the devil: and the harvest is the end of the world; and the reapers are angels." In the Diaglott version, which gives the original Greek and a word-for-word translation, this reads: "THAT ENEMY who SOWED them is the ADVERSARY; the HARVEST is the End of the Age; and the REAPERS are Messengers." In this as in many other passages where Jesus used the word "age," it has been translated "world," leading the reader to believe that Jesus taught that this planet was to be destroyed.

So we see that the almost universally accepted teaching of the end of the world is not properly founded on the Bible. The translators wanted to give the wicked a great scare, so they put "the end of the world" into Jesus' mouth in several instances where He plainly said "the end of the age."

The Bible is a textbook of absolute Truth; but its teachings are veiled in symbol and understood only by the illumined.

In accordance with the prophecies of the ancients, our planetary system has just completed a journey of 2,169 years, in which there has been wonderful material progress without its spiritual counterpart. But old conditions have passed away and a new era has dawned. A great change is taking place in the mentality of the race, and this change is evidenced in literature, science, and religion. There is a breaking away from old creeds and old doctrines, and there is a tendency to form centers along lines of scientific spiritual thought. The literature of the first half of the twentieth century is so saturated with occultism as to be an object of censure by conservatives, who denounce it as a "lapse into the superstition of the past." Notwithstanding the protests of the conservatives, on every hand are evidences of spiritual freedom; it crops out in so many ways that an enumeration would cover the whole field of life.

It is evident that Jesus and His predecessors had knowledge of coming events on lines of such absolute accuracy as to place it in the realm of truth ascertained, that is, exact science.

Do you belong to the old, or are you building anew from within and keeping time with the progress of the age? The "harvest" or "consummation of the age" pointed out by Jesus is not far off. This is no theological scare; it is a statement based on a law that is now being tested and proved.

Listen to your inner voice; cultivate the good, the pure, the God within you. Do not let your false beliefs keep you in the darkness of error until you go out like a dying ember. The divine spark is within you. Fan it into flame by right thinking, right living, and right doing, and you will find the "new Jerusalem."

One of the pioneering leaders of the New Thought movement, CHARLES FILLMORE (1884–1948), with his wife Myrtle, founded the worldwide Unity ministry. An early visionary in using mass media to spread religious and inspirational messages, Fillmore was widely known for his metaphysical interpretations of the Bible, and for his books including *Prosperity; Christian Healing; Talks on Truth; Atom-Smashing Power of Mind*; and *The Twelve Powers.*

MITCH HOROWITZ is the PEN Award-winning author of books including *Occult America* and *The Miracle Club.* A writer-in-residence at the New York Public Library and lecturer-in-residence at the University of Philosophical Research in Los Angeles, Mitch introduces and edits G&D Media's line of Condensed Classics and is the author of the Napoleon Hill Success Course series, including *The Miracle of a Definite Chief Aim* and *The Power of the Master Mind.* Visit him at MitchHorowitz.com.